Success With

Numbers & Concepts

SCHOLASTIC

Editor: Ourania Papacharalambous
Cover design by Tannaz Fassihi; cover illustration by Kevin Zimmer
Interior design by Mina Chen
Interior illustrations by Gabriele Tafuni (11, 38); Gareth Conway (21, 22, 33, 43, 45);
Carol Herring (27); Doug Jones (spot art)
All other images © Shutterstock.com

ISBN 978-1-338-79857-9
Scholastic Inc., 557 Broadway, New York, NY 10012
Copyright © 2022 Scholastic Inc.
All rights reserved. Printed in the U.S.A.
First printing, January 2022
1 2 3 4 5 6 7 8 9 10   40   29 28 27 26 25 24 23 22

INTRODUCTION

Parents and teachers alike will find *Scholastic Success With Numbers & Concepts* to be a valuable learning tool. Children will enjoy completing a wide variety of math activities that are both engaging and educational. The activities include mazes, hidden pictures, matching, and other fun ways to learn about basic math concepts. While engaged in these activities, children practice recognizing and counting numbers from 1 to 20. They will also learn about one-to-one correspondence, identify number words from one to twenty, and solve problems using pictures. On page 4, you will find a list of the key skills covered in the activities throughout this book. You will feel rewarded providing such a valuable resource for your children.

TABLE OF CONTENTS

Key Skills 4

Circle and Square Search *(Identify shapes)* 5

Rectangle and Triangle Teasers *(Identify shapes)* 6

Oval and Diamond Detectives *(Identify shapes)* 7

Shape Match-Up *(Identify shapes)* 8

More Shape Match-Up *(Identify shapes)* 9

Shape Teasers *(Identify shapes)* 10

Zany Shapes *(Identify shapes)* 11

1, 2 . . . Presents for You!
(Identify groups of 1 and 2 objects) 12

3, 4 . . . Let's Read More!
(Identify groups of 3 and 4 objects) 13

5, 6 . . . Flowers to Pick!
(Identify groups of 5 and 6 objects) 14

7, 8 . . . Time to Skate!
(Identify groups of 7 and 8 objects) 15

9, 10 . . . It's Fun to Win!
(Identify groups of 9 and 10 objects) 16

Bunny Number Fun *(Identify numbers 1–9)* 17

A Colorful Garden
(Count groups of 1–9 objects) 18

Gumball Goodies
(Count groups of 2–10 objects) 19

Count and Color *(Count groups of 1–10 objects)* 20

Calling All Alarms *(Order numbers from 1 to 10)* 21

11, 12 . . . It's on the Shelf!
(Identify groups of 11 and 12 objects) 22

13, 14 . . . Let's Play the Tambourine!
(Identify groups of 13 and 14 objects) 23

15, 16 . . . Eat Your Peas!
(Identify groups of 15 and 16 objects) 24

17, 18 . . . Don't Forget the Sunscreen!
(Identify groups of 17 and 18 objects) 25

19, 20 . . . There Are Plenty!
(Identify groups of 19 and 20 objects) 26

Time to Build *(Identify numbers 11–20)* 27

Let's Count! *(Count groups of 11–18 objects)* 28

Fun Fruits *(Count groups of 13–20 objects)* 29

Flying High *(Count groups of 11–20 objects)* 30

Juggling Act *(Order numbers from 1 to 20)* 31

Each Number in Its Spot
(Order numbers from 11 to 20) 32

Pick Up Trash! *(Order numbers from 1 to 20)* 33

Keep on Trucking *(Order numbers from 1 to 20)* 34

Counting Windows *(Order numbers from 1 to 20)* 35

Smiling Shapes *(Identify patterns)* 36

What Comes Next? *(Identify patterns)* 37

Decorate a Headband *(Identify patterns)* 38

Look-Alikes *(Identify equal groups)* 39

Just the Same *(Identify equal groups)* 40

Tasty Treats *(Count/More than)* 41

A Little Snack *(Count/Fewer than)* 42

Sweet Spotted Buddies *(Count/More than)* 43

Moving Along *(Solve problems using pictures)* 44

A Perfect Day at the Park
(Solve problems using pictures) 45

Easy as One, Two, Three
(Identify number words 1–10) 46

Busy Bees *(Identify number words 11–20)* 47

Lovely, Little Ladybugs
(Identify number words 1–20) 48

Grade-Appropriate Skills Covered in *Scholastic Success With Numbers & Concepts*

Know number names and the count sequence.

Count forward beginning from a given number within the known sequence.

Write numbers from 0 to 20. Represent a number of objects with a written numeral 0–20.

Count to tell the number of objects.

Understand the relationship between numbers and quantities; connect counting to cardinality.

When counting objects, say the number names in the standard order, pairing each object with one and only one number name and each number name with one and only one object.

Understand that the last number name said tells the number of objects counted. The number of objects is the same regardless of their arrangement or the order in which they were counted.

Understand that each successive number name refers to a quantity that is one larger.

Count to answer "how many?" questions about as many as 20 things arranged in a line, a rectangular array, or a circle, or as many as 10 things in a scattered configuration; given a number from 1–20, count out that many objects.

Identify whether the number of objects in one group is greater than, less than, or equal to the number of objects in another group.

Compare two numbers between 1 and 10 presented as written numerals.

Solve addition and subtraction word problems, and add and subtract within 10.

Fluently add and subtract within 5.

Identify and describe shapes.

Correctly name shapes regardless of their orientations or overall size.

Analyze, compare, create, and compose shapes.

Model shapes in the world by building shapes from components and drawing shapes.

Circle and Square Search

Color each circle shape.

Color each square shape.

Rectangle and Triangle Teasers

Color each rectangle shape.

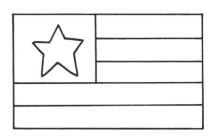

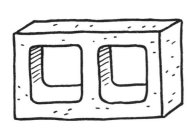

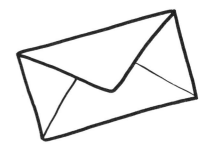

Color each triangle shape.

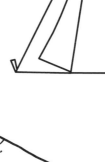

Oval and Diamond Detectives

Color each diamond shape.

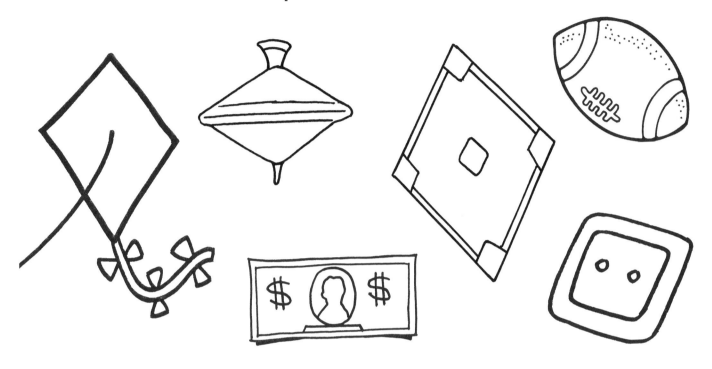

Color each oval shape.

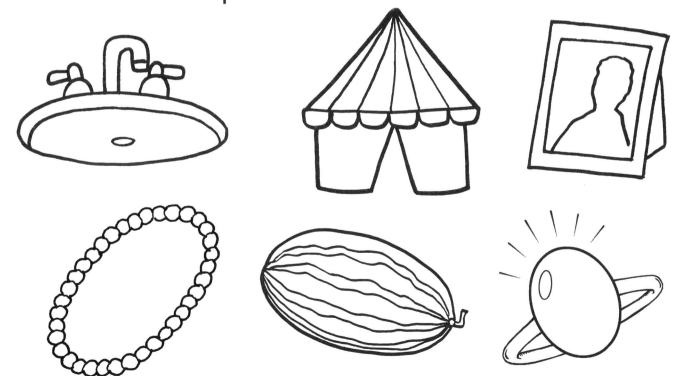

Shape Match-Up

Trace each shape. Draw a line to match each object to its shape. Color.

More Shape Match-Up

Trace each shape. Draw a line to match each object to its shape. Color.

square

oval

diamond

rectangle

Shape Teasers

Color each shape. Use the color key.

red   ▲ blue   ■ green   ■ yellow

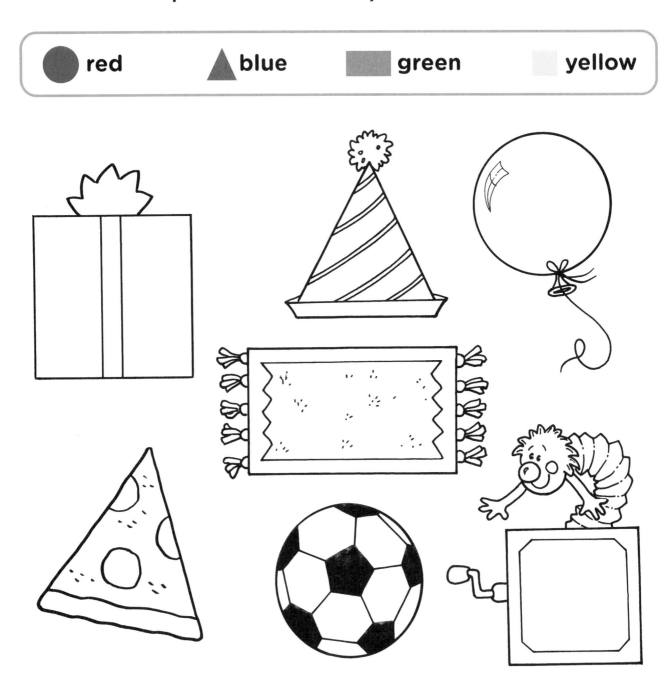

 Name something else with each shape.

Zany Shapes

Color each shape in the picture. Use the color key.

♦ black ▪ blue ▲ red
▬ brown ● green ⬭ orange

1, 2...Presents for You!

**Draw a circle around each group of 1.
Draw a square around each group of 2.**

3, 4... Let's Read More!

Draw a triangle around each group of 3.
Draw a diamond around each group of 4.

Scholastic Success With Numbers & Concepts   **13**

5, 6... Flowers to Pick!

Draw an oval around each group of 5.
Draw a rectangle around each group of 6.

7, 8... Time to Skate!

Color each group of 7 red. Color each group of 8 yellow.

9, 10... It's Fun to Win!

Color each group of 9 blue. Color each group of 10 green.

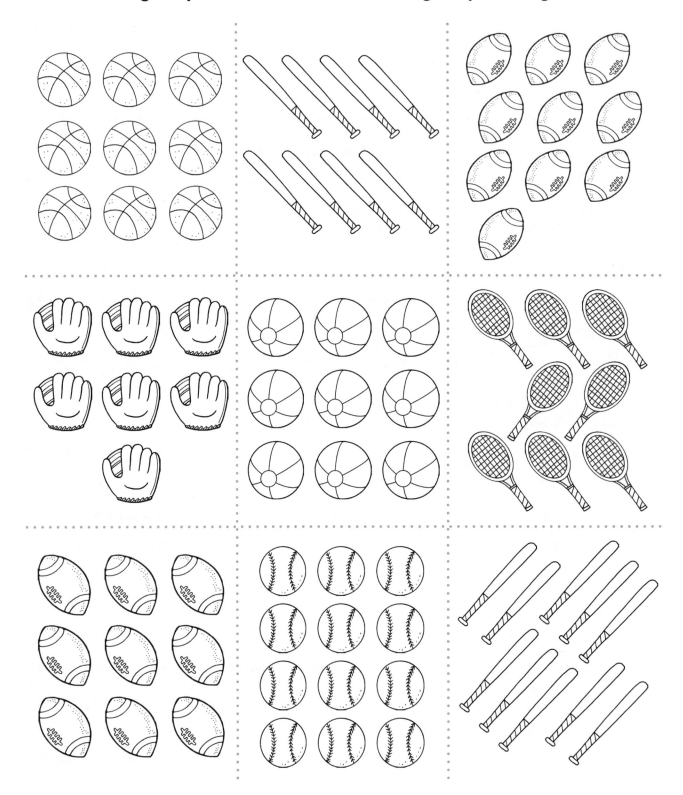

© Scholastic Inc.

Bunny Number Fun

Use the color key to color the picture.

1 pink	2 green	3 blue	4 red	5 brown
6 yellow	7 purple	8 black	9 orange	

A Colorful Garden

Use the color key to color the picture.

yellow : pink : red :: black :: orange

:: purple :: blue :::: green ::: brown

© Scholastic Inc.

Gumball Goodies

Use the color key to color the picture.

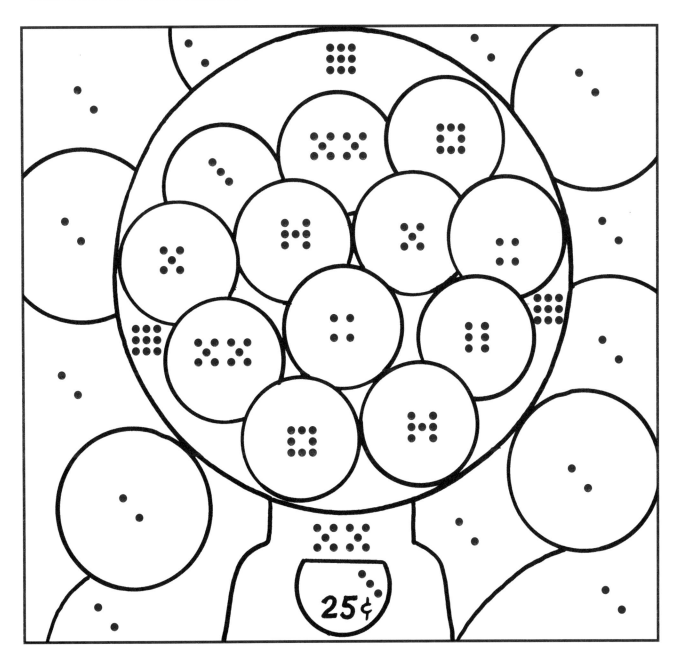

Count and Color

Color the correct number of objects in each row.

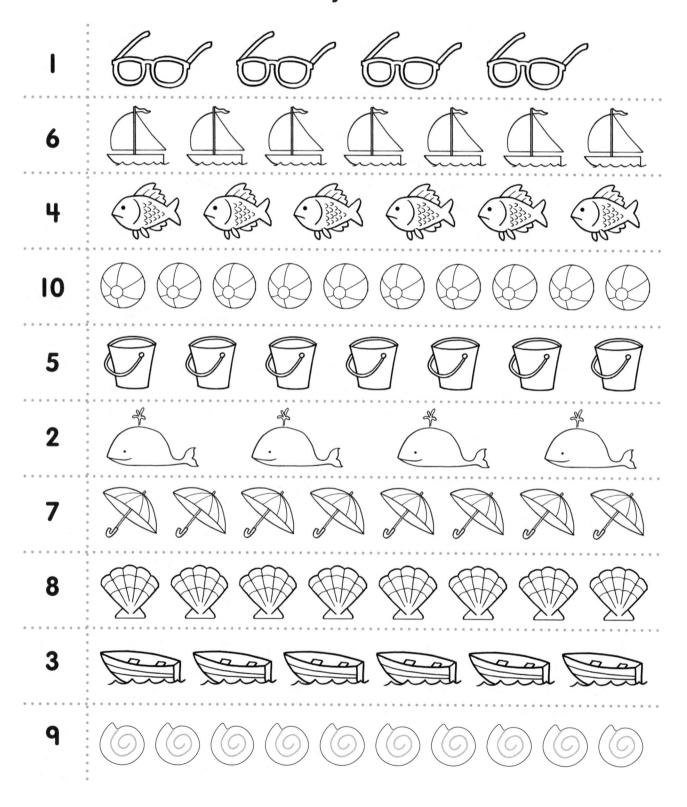

Calling All Alarms

Help the fire truck get to the fire.
Color the path that goes in order from 1 to 10.

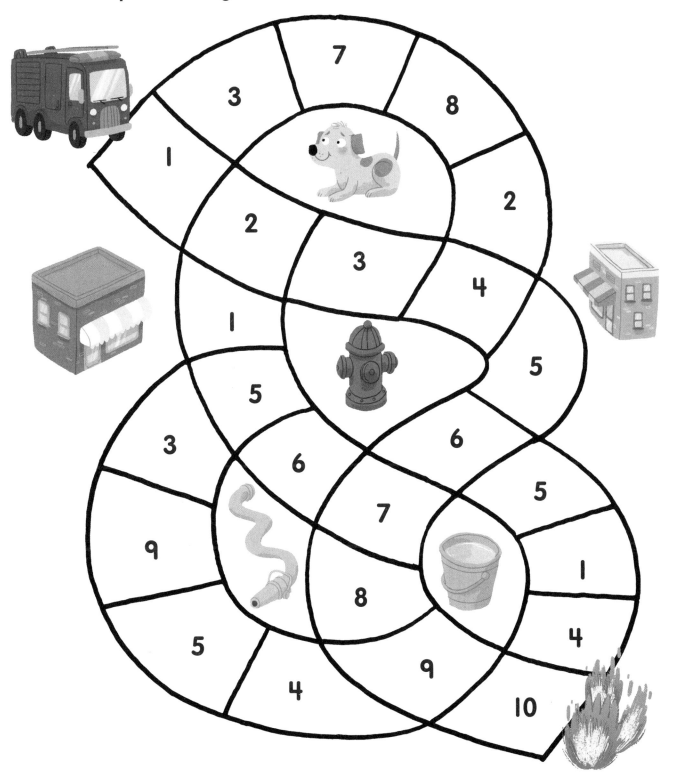

11, 12... It's on the Shelf!

Draw a circle around each group of 11.
Draw a square around each group of 12.

13, 14... Let's Play the Tambourine!

Draw an oval around each group of 13.
Draw a rectangle around each group of 14.

 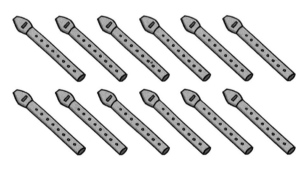

15, 16… Eat Your Peas!

Draw a circle around each group of 15.
Draw a rectangle around each group of 16.

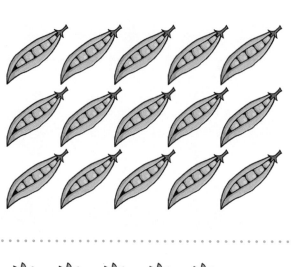

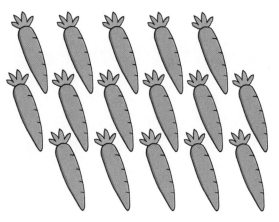

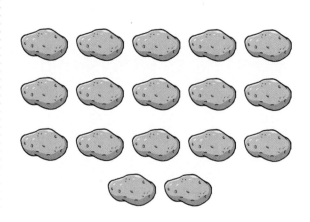

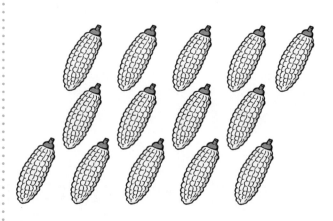

17, 18...Don't Forget the Sunscreen!

Draw a circle around each group of 17.
Draw a square around each group of 18.

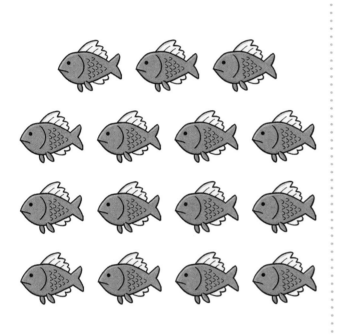

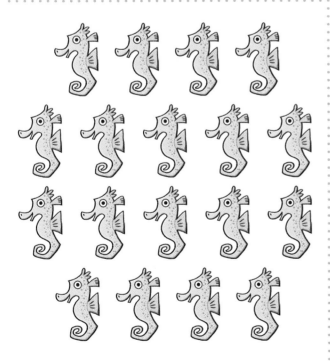

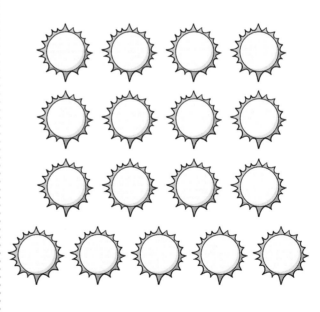

19, 20 . . . There Are Plenty!

Draw a circle around each group of 19.
Draw a square around each group of 20.

Time to Build

Use the color key to color the picture.

11 yellow	**12** black	**13** blue	**14** white	**15** orange
16 green	**17** red	**18** purple	**19** brown	**20** pink

Let's Count!

Color the correct number of objects in each row.

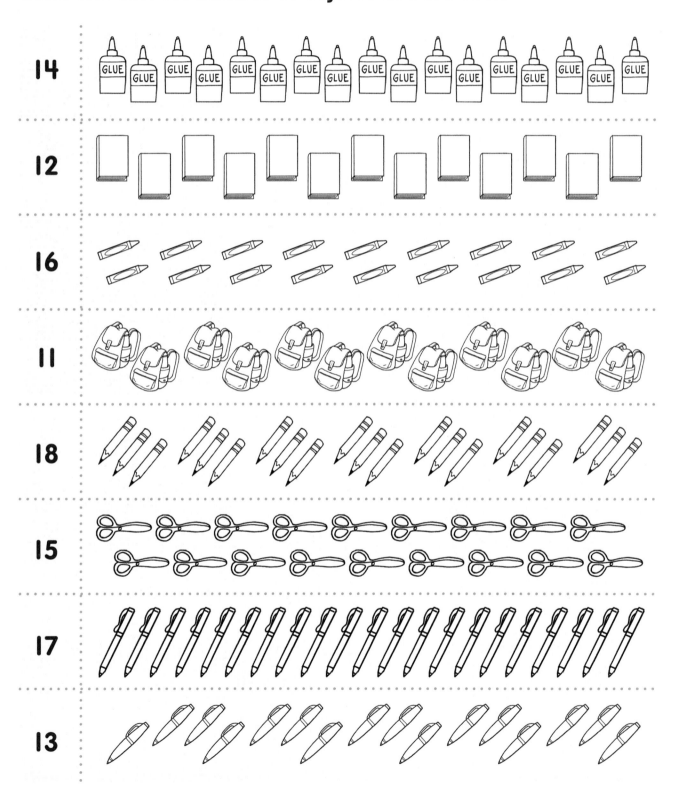

14

12

16

11

18

15

17

13

Fun Fruits

Count each group of fruit. Draw a line to the matching numbers.

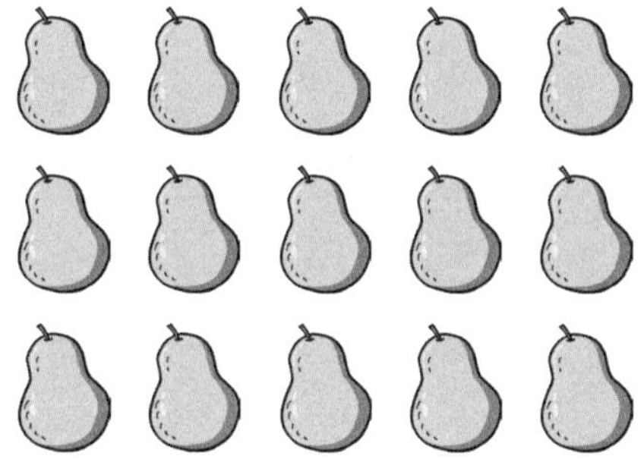

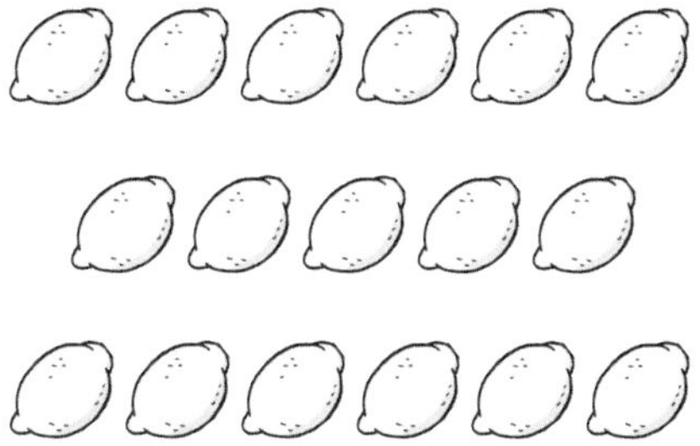

13

14

15

16

17

18

19

20

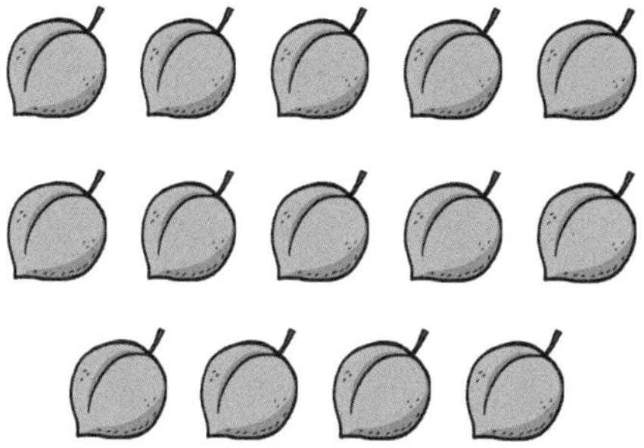

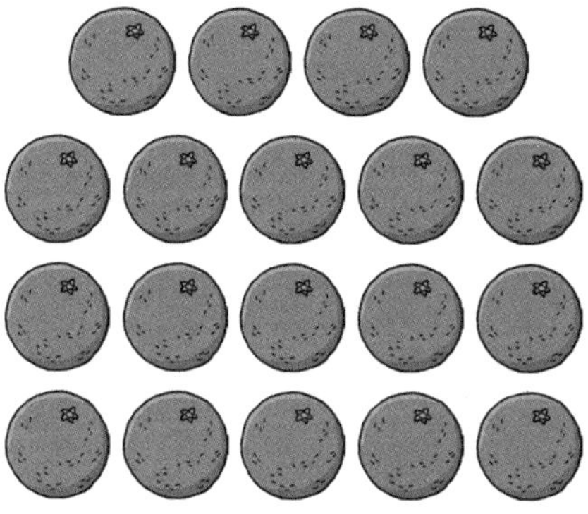

Scholastic Success With Numbers & Concepts   **29**

Flying High

Color the bows on the tails to match the number above each kite.

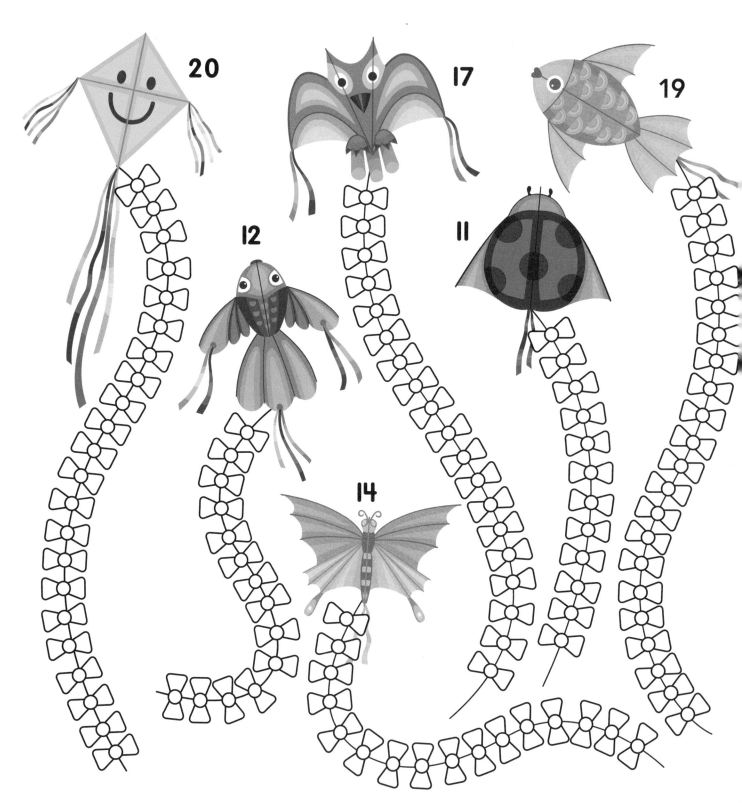

Juggling Act

Write each missing number.

Each Number in Its Spot

Write each missing number.

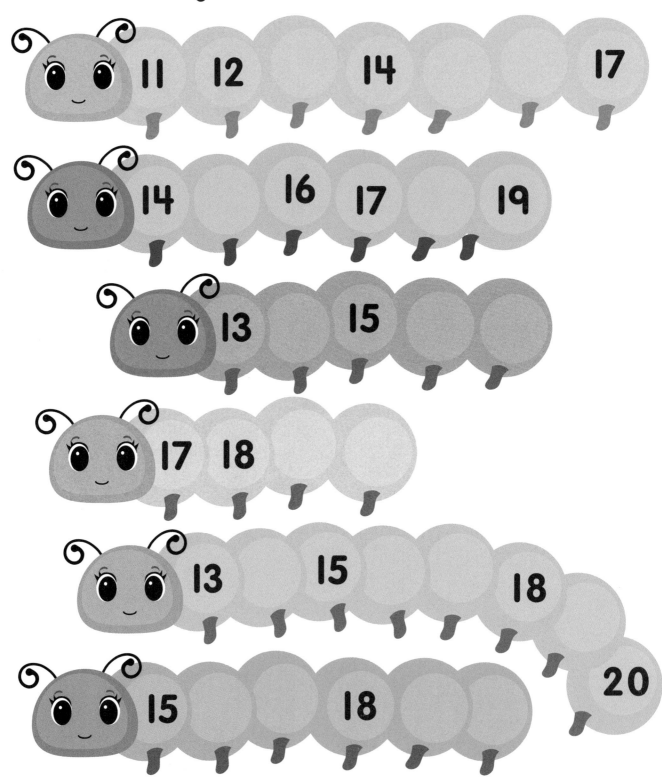

Pick Up Trash!

Help the trash collector find his way to the trash can.
Color a path in order from 1 to 20.

START

Keep on Trucking

Connect the dots from 1 to 20.

© Scholastic Inc.

Counting Windows

Write the missing numbers.

Smiling Shapes

What shape is next in each pattern? Draw a line to match it.

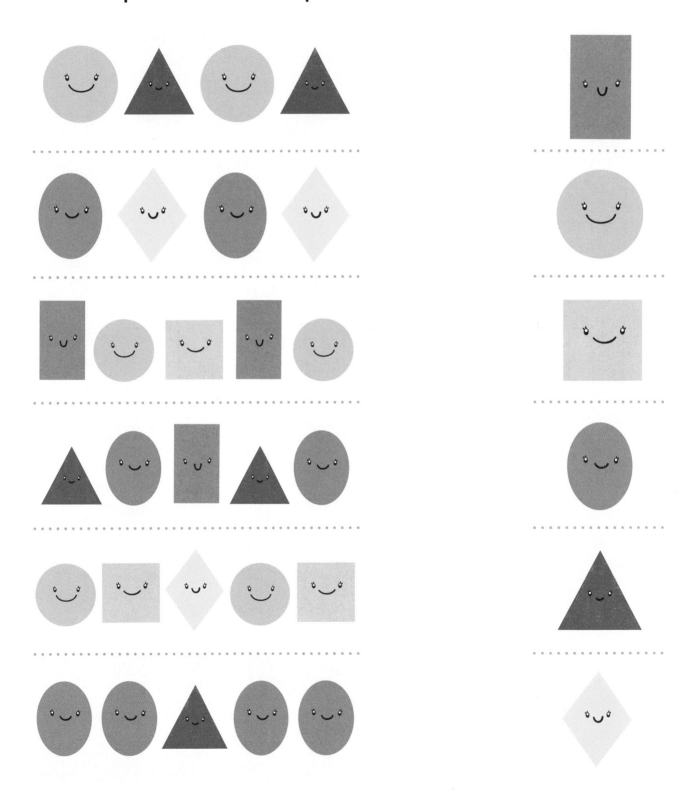

What Comes Next?

What shape is next in each pattern? Circle it.

Decorate a Headband

Draw shapes to finish each pattern. Then color the headbands.

Look-Alikes

Color the pictures with the same number as the first picture.

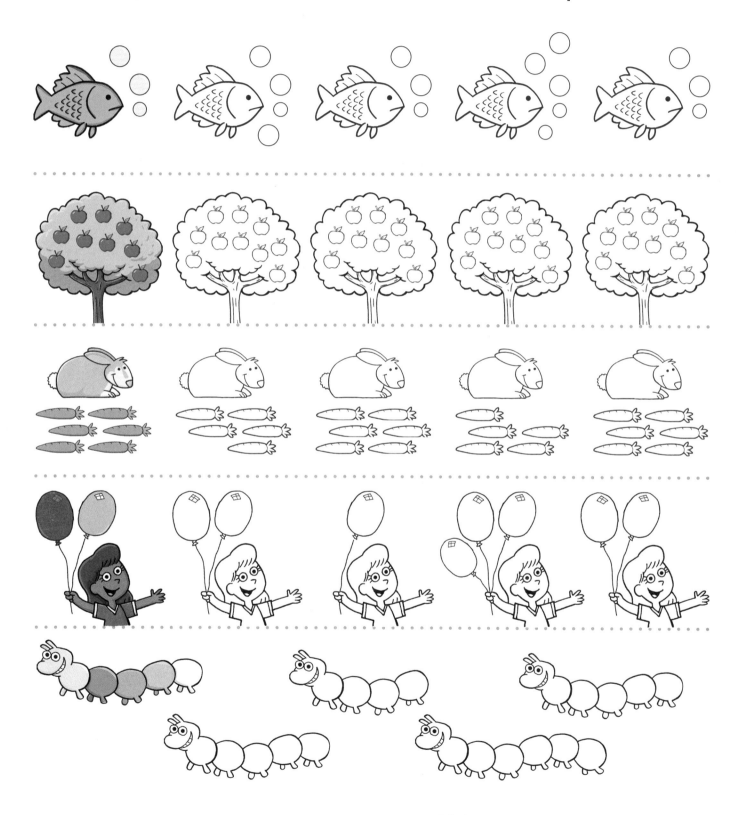

Just the Same

Draw a line to match the groups with the same number of items.

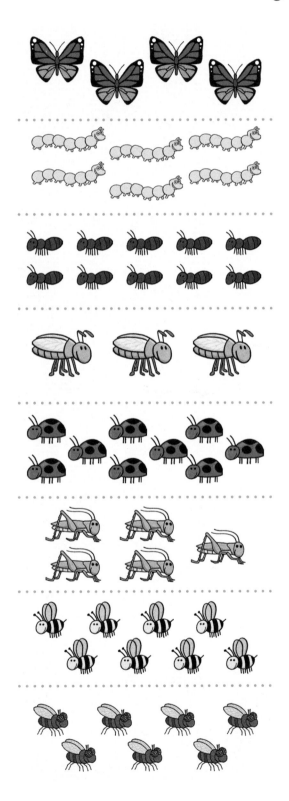
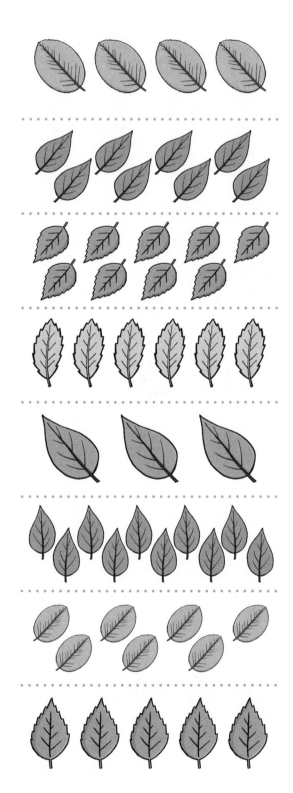

Tasty Treats

Circle the one with more.

A Little Snack

Circle the one with **fewer**.

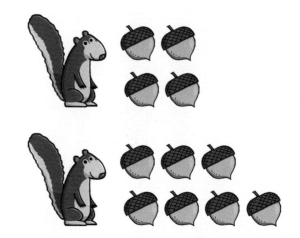

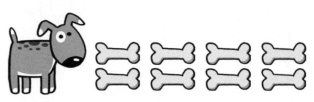

Sweet Spotted Buddies

In each picture, color the dog with more spots.

Moving Along

Look at the picture.

Write the number. How many?

How many in all?

 and     and

 and   and

 and   and

A Perfect Day at the Park

Circle how many of each you see in the picture.

 1   5

 4   2

 8   5

 6   3

 7   10

 2   8

 9   7

 10   7

 3   1

Circle how many you see in all.

 + =   8   9   10

 + =   3   8   9

 + =   6   2   4

Easy as One, Two, Three

Use the color key to color the picture.

one = yellow	**two** = black	**three** = blue	**four** = white
five = orange	**six** = green	**seven** = red	**eight** = purple
nine = brown	**ten** = pink		

Busy Bees

Count the bees in each picture. Circle the correct number word.

Lovely, Little Ladybugs

Count the spots on each ladybug. Circle the correct number word.

one

five

two

seven

fourteen

sixteen

nineteen

fifteen

ten

eleven

twenty

twelve

eighteen

thirteen

nine

eight

seven

four

seven

three